HOW TO HUN

RABBITS, DUCKS, DEER, BEAR, CATFISH, TUNA, SHARK & MORE

BY VINCE STEAD

How to Hunt & Fish for Rabbits, Ducks, Deer, Bear, Catfish, Tuna, Shark & More

www.VinceStead.com

1. HOW TO GO RABBIT HUNTING

It's not hard to locate the right spots for rabbit hunting. Wherever there are plenty of rabbits, you can be sure there is an abundant food supply available nearby, and you know rabbits would thrive really well there. The best places to search for rabbits would be by bushes, the woods, briars, fencerows and even alongside drainage systems. A densely covered rail line or places to hide would also have rabbits thriving there, so check out those places as well. You should not ignore old farmhouses, or irrigation pipes on the ground, as rabbits like to live in them also.

The best way to locate rabbits would be to drive down early in the morning or late at night on the rural routes, and you would find many rabbits running around. Now that you know where to look for the rabbits, let's find out how you can hunt for them now.

You can hunt for many rabbits when you have the right rifle with you, a .22 rifle that is, some even use a bow and arrow, or even a pistol for hunting rabbits. You could also choose to use a shotgun, a 20 gauge that has an improved cylinder choke. Now while you are busy thinking of shooting rabbits, ensure you are well covered and protected or else the thorns and briars along the path rabbits like to hide could hurt you.

If you are lucky enough to own a Beagle, they make some of the best rabbit hunting dogs to have. Beagles will happily go sniffing the trails and will follow the chase and bring the hunt back to you. Their barks would be like angels playing the harp on a cold winter morning, while they bark their ways to the rabbit and bring it to the ground and finally to you, since most rabbits will run in a circle.

If you don't have a Beagle or a pack of them, then you should wait out the rabbits, which is the traditional way of rabbit hunting. In this situation, you need to be camouflaged and wait patiently until you out wait the rabbits. If you pause at any given point of time, the rabbit would pick up the signs and take off for their life. Choose a location suitable for hunting and walk slowly. The ideal thumb rule is 10:30, paces to seconds that is. This would make the rabbits think they have been spotted and when you pause silently, they start to run.

Snap shooting is the best way for rabbit hunting, say experts. Rabbits wouldn't wait for you to shoot them and they don't have the time to swing around where you would want to target them. It is up to you now to locate the prey and shoot in an instant.

The best thing about rabbit hunting is that you don't need to have props or blinds set up to hunt. All you have to do is have many quick senses in place and patience to hunt down your rabbit.

2. HOW TO GO DUCK HUNTING

There are all sorts of hobbies and activities that one can conduct during their free time. Depending on your interest and personality, the activities you would be pursuing might be different, even amongst your friends. Some activities are common whereas some may not be. For instance, duck hunting is one of those activities that many would assume that it is filled with unknowns and complicated methods. No matter if, you are interested with this hunting activity or you have been ducking hunting before, some of these guidelines here might be useful for you to try out yourself in the near future.

Before heading out the door for duck hunting, always make sure that you are having all the necessary tools and equipment for this activity. One of the equipment's you should not overlook is waders, especially for individuals who do not wish to get their bodies' wet while duck hunting. Of course, although a set of waders might be expensive, do not fret that you might waste the money-buying waders if you do not plan to go duck hunting for a long time. You can still use your waders for any other fishing activities and also to keep yourself warm during any outdoor activities, do go ahead and buy some.

Of course, ducks will never march their ways towards you when you are merely hunting them. By this, you would definitely need some extra help from the decoys. Many would prefer to use a robot duck, which you will be able to obtain in the market for an affordable price, to lure the ducks out. The robot duck is believed to be one of the most effective decoys to tempt the ducks out of their hiding places. Apart from that, you can also use the technique of duck calls to further enhance the effectiveness of luring the ducks out. Duck calls are like a push to persuade the ducks to come towards you, and it is best used when your decoys seem to be providing slow and fruitless results.

Now you know the important equipment you should bring along when duck hunting. The next thing you need to know about duck hunting is the best locations to conduct the hunt. There are a few factors you can put into consideration when selecting the best places for duck hunting. It is better for you to look out for big pools or big water areas. In order to find out where the ducks will be spending most of their time, you need to be attentive of the weather patterns as well as the water levels of the water area.

Furthermore, if you are planning to conduct duck hunting for a long period of time, it is also recommended for you to keep a hunting log, jotting down the necessary information every time you go duck hunting so that it would be easier for you to track down the best locations the next time you go duck hunting.

3. HOW TO GO DUCK HUNTING #2

The best time to go duck hunting as most experts say would be early season. However, call it luck or strategy, because here are some key points to remember before you go duck hunting.

Where are some of the best places to go duck hunting? For those of you who are hunting ducks, you need to identify the areas. Areas such as potholes, backwater bays, open water areas, large open water spaces, pools, areas which have smartweed or even duckweed etc. are the best places to check for ducks. You could also look for areas where heavy food quantities would be available, such as areas filled with smartweed or even millet to name a few.

If there were new spaces or fringes, which have been recently flooded, you would find ducks habituating those places as well. Also, check backwater timer areas and areas where there is dense cover as well.

The duck decoy you use, should match the duck you hunt. A decoy would help you bring down the ducks you aim to shoot. The best way to do this is to have a spread of mixed decoys scattered all over. This way you would have various species of ducks coming to you, the more the merrier they say.

Small groups for decoys spreading are necessary. Don't put all your decoys in one place; spread them around in groups not too big. The thumb rule is 2 to 7 decoys, which should be 2 to 3 feet away from one another. Do this all around the area, which you plan to hunt in. Remember, in the early season, ducks don't gather together and move together, so take advantage of these phenomena and spread the decoys appropriately.

The calls for early season duck hunting should be subtle. In the early season, the ducks aren't too loud and vociferous. Do not be aggressive when calling the ducks, you could instead use peeps, chuckles, quacks, or drake mallard calls, which would be these birds closer to you.

Blend in with the surrounding. Don't use camouflage patterns when the early season is off, it doesn't work with duck hunting. Dead grass shades and light browns are a flop when they mix with darker or lighter shades of green. The best thing would be to attach some foliage to your camouflage and use deer or turkey camouflage to go duck hunting during the mid-seasons.

Smaller shots and wider chokes. Remember, during the early season the ducks would move fast, hence targeting them wouldn't be easy. The choke size should thus be increased and a shotgun shell should be used, size 4 or more is the best.

4. HOW TO PHEASANT HUNTING

Depending on your personality and your interest, there are many activities you can choose to pursue during your free time. Individuals who prefer an escapade into the fictional world will habitually choose to read books or watch movies when they are free whereas individuals who are adventurous and outgoing would generally take part in some outdoor activities, which are often challenging. If you are an outgoing and adventurous person, you might be interested with this outdoor activity called pheasant hunting.

Pheasant hunting, similar to duck hunting, is one activity that is good for you to spend your free time doing something electrifying, and also to help you with the building up of your stamina. If you are very new to pheasant hunting, this will give you a brief idea of what you should know about pheasant hunting to prepare yourself for this exciting and amusing activity.

First of all, pheasant hunting is definitely not an easy task for everyone. It is not easy to lure those alerting pheasants to come out from their hiding places as you please. Thus, it is important for you to bring along a guide for your first few times of pheasant hunting. One of the best guides you can take along is a dog. However, you would need to train your dog first before marching straight into pheasant hunting. Dogs are one of the best guides for you to use because of their natural instincts, which will assist you detecting the locations of the pheasants almost instantly.

Secondly, it is also extremely important for you to be as quiet as possible when you approach one location, which possibly has some pheasants. Pheasants are sensitive creatures, which are extremely attentive to their surroundings. Slamming a car door or the sounds of footsteps can easily chase them away. Thus, what you need to do is to approach the pheasants as quietly as possible, with unhurried and stable footsteps to keep them unknown to your presence.

If you are thinking of how many people should you invite to join you for some pheasant hunting, it is recommended that the more the better. With more pheasant hunters, it also means that the area you will be covering will be larger, and thus, increasing the possible capturing rate for you and your friends. In the same time, if possible, it would be great if you were able to keep a hunting log for yourself, jotting down the necessary information whenever you go for any pheasant hunting. This is important for you to discover the routines of the pheasants so that you can further plan your pheasant hunting to be more fruitful.

It is also recommended that you keep your body in shape first before you march out for more pheasant hunting activity. Pheasant hunting is not an easy activity to be conducted and it involves a lot of walking up and down and under the unpleasant weather conditions sometimes. Thus, to ensure that you can obtain the most excitement out of the activity, always make sure that you are physically in pretty good shape.

5. How to go Pheasant Hunting #2

Pheasant hunting can be great and a fun filled activity to enjoy in the great outdoors. However, there are certain few things to bear in mind when going pheasant hunting.

You need to have a good bird dog with you, especially if this is your first time.
Don't forget your shotgun. Roam the hunting area making an S pattern, so that you leave no ground uncovered. Your bird dog would be the best guide, he would tell you with his sniffs where to stop and when he does, you will be able to shoot suddenly.

The dog would retrieve the catch and bring it to you. Notice the flight of the bird and then take aim; this is when the bird is above your height and it is when you should shoot. You don't have much time, just barely a few seconds and you have to be fast to be successful at pheasant hunting.

Before you go out pheasant hunting, try shooting clay pigeons to practice your target shooting. It is important you have a good bird dog for company and help, as he will help you flush it out when the shooting is done.

You need to be fit and strong for pheasant hunting,

and it will drain some of your energy out in no time, especially when you have to walk and climb hills a lot to have the right areas to hunt and kill.

The gun safety should always be on when you are taking aim and getting ready to shoot. Remember to disengage the gun safety before you shoot, especially when you are getting closer to the target.

If you are pheasant hunting in a group, walk in one straight line so you don't shoot one another. If someone misses a target, don't scream and yell or else the birds fly away?
Safety should always be a priority when pheasant hunting is going on, you shouldn't play with your gun or you could kill your dog or shoot someone accidentally.

Your gun should be clean and properly maintained and ready to go. The bird shouldn't be killed on the ground, for there would be bird sprays that shoot out. Always use the help of an experienced pheasant hunter that's if you are doing this for the first time. Safety is necessary, stay calm and composed while you go for the kill, impatience would lead to nothing. Have fun and engage others with motivational talks, but don't be too loud or aggressive, or else you will shoo away the birds and pheasant hunting would turn out to be a day with no pheasants to take home.

6. How to Go Raccoon Hunting

The pace of society will directly influence the workload of an individual and their precious free time for hobbies like raccoon hunting. Today, the workload on working individuals is definitely heavier than what they used to be. However, no matter how busy an individual is, he or she should never forget to forge out some of his or her time to relax him or herself so that he or she can prepare to fight for a longer journey ahead. There are many activities one can conduct during his and her free time. If you are looking for some challenging activity, maybe you can try out raccoon hunting.

Raccoon hunting is recommended for individuals who are outgoing and are constantly looking for some adventure in their life. Here are some guidelines for you to get you started with your raccoon hunting activity. Before you start off, be sure to apply for a license for raccoon hunting. Heading off for any raccoon, hunting activity without a license is considered illegal and can be penalized by the local government. If you want to know about the permits or licenses you need to apply for, in order for you to carry out this activity, you may check with your local government.

After obtaining the necessary license or permit, you may now begin. However, your raccoon hunting may not be successful without a raccoon-hunting dog. The raccoon-hunting dog plays an important role in guiding you to locate the raccoons in the wild accurately. Without the raccoon hunting dog, you might end up searching in the wrong location and returning empty handed.

If you are unsure about the suitable time for you to go raccoon hunting, the recommended time here is during the nighttime. This is because raccoons are nocturnal and they often come out from their hiding places to hunt for food at nighttime. In short, the raccoons usually conduct their activities at night instead of during the daytime. Another advantage for you when you conduct raccoon hunting at night is that the possibility for you to be noticed by the raccoons will be decreased.

To make your raccoon hunting easier, it is also advisable for you to conduct some research beforehand in finding out the feeding spots of the raccoons, as well as their homes and the trees they use to climb. There are also the options of using traps to capture the raccoons, which is one of the favorite techniques preferred by most raccoon hunters. The raccoon traps come in different forms and types. The most commonly used raccoon trap is the cage.

In addition, it is important for you to ensure that you have equipped yourself with the most appropriate tools before you head out for your raccoon hunting activity. If you are hunting at night, be sure to bring along enough lighting to enable you to see your way and your targets. In the same time, it is also advisable for you to bring the tools or equipment, which can help you increase your efficiency of raccoon hunting.

7. How to go for opossum hunting

The most significant thing you can do when it comes to opossum hunting is tracking an opossum. It becomes very important to learn how to trap opossums. Trapping opossums involves many techniques.

Luring opossums: Recent few surveys conducted by Wildlife NGOs reveals that opossums are very greedy by nature. Using these characteristics of them, trapping opossums becomes much easier. They may be lured by baiting with spices being mixed with flour. At times oil essences are also used. It may be mentioned here that opossums have great eyesight, which betrays them by attracting the opossums towards silver objects. The hunters use this weakness of the opossums too in opossum hunting.

Leg traps: It is the most popular methods that are generally adopted by the hunters during opossum hunting. What the hunters exactly do is that they set a leg trap lured by the baits so that the trap comes in the way of the opossum's run and hence they are trapped.

A precautionary measure that is taken care of when using the trap is that leg trap is set in such a position that an opossum when trapped is hanged on to it. Besides the traps may also be set at a 45° to any tree available so that non-target animals are not trapped in the set leg trap.

Cage traps: Cages are also used when it comes to opossum hunting. When cage traps are used, the doors of the cage should be checked properly. The baits installed in it should be taken care of and most significantly, the cage trap set up should be checked at least once in 2 to 3 days so that all remains good! Trapping opossums is not the only part that plays the lead in opossum hunting.

Hunting methods too are far more important when it comes to opossum hunting. When describing the methods, there are mainly three types, poison, shooting and trapping.

For some reason, if you have to use poison, the best poisons used are 1080, cyanide, phosphorus, pin done etc. If you are out shooting opossums, you will need a firearm license. A 0.22 caliber rifle is the most popular, as it ensures the stability of the skins and hides as well as the meat.

8. How To Go Deer Hunting

You would have a different experience altogether going deer hunting, but it is a tough experience so be ready for all the challenges. To go deer hunting, there are many things to keep in mind.

The first thing you should do is to get a permit from the local environment and wildlife authorities. Check what the state laws where you live have to say about deer hunting, remember it differs from one state to another, especially about owning firearms and hunting equipment. Don't play around with the law, or else you would be hunted down yourself by law enforcement.

Deer hunting is best enjoyed in groups, but bring along responsible family and friends for the same. However, if you choose to have the hunting experience done on a solo basis, ensure you have a cell phone with a full charge with you. Also inform your family of the location you would be hunting at, and when you plan to come back home. Ask someone to now and then check on your safety, carry a GPS if you don't know the location well, a topographical map would help as well.

You should also have the right pair of hunting boots to wear, it should be waterproof and your feet shouldn't be cold while the hunting is going on. In addition, you should have a "hot seat" to keep your behind warm while you sit and wait for the deer to pass; this is to be used only if the weather is cold, snowy or rainy.

Go with an experienced hunter, if this is your first time. It is not only for the learning experience, but would also keep you safe. Learn about the hunting laws in the area you live in or the state for that matter. Check for hunting signs when you venture out. For example, rubs, scrapes and even game trails, which would tell you where the deer frequent all too often.

Use different spots when hunting, the deer movements and habits are constantly changing during the hunting season, due to the weather and even human impact on their living space. Use the help of deer calls, if you are a novice it would be wise to have an experienced hunter help you with the same.

Deer have amazing sense of smell and can tell from a human odor to an animal, so use cover scent. Camouflaging is important and so is the need for a flashlight, which is good. When you shoot the deer, watch it fall and wait. Then along with a friend drag it out of the spot and out of the woods.

Finally, don't shoot the first deer that comes along your way, wait for the right one, you will know it.

9. How to Go Moose Hunting

There are many types of activities and hobbies we can choose to conduct during our free times. We can choose to go for the common ones such as reading, watching movies, and so on. Nowadays, activities, which are more challenging and exciting, are also getting more attention from individuals. One of these unique activities includes the hobby of moose hunting.

No matter if, you are a skilled moose hunter or a moose hunter with barely any experience, your goals are always the same, to gain the most out of the moose hunting experience. Certain guidelines will be listed in order to help you optimize your moose hunting skills and in the same time, assisting you to gain the most out of your moose hunting adventure.

The first thumb of rule for moose hunting is to concentrate only in one area. Although the location you had chosen for moose hunting might be a very huge area, it might be better for you to focus on one area instead of going around the whole area hunting for the moose, which its location is still unknown to you. Apart from that, you might also want to consider using a moose call as part of your technique for moose hunting. Using a moose call can help you in luring the moose out of their hiding places, which they might assume that the comrades are calling them, thus, falling into the trap you had set.

If the location you had chosen for any moose hunting activity is too huge, it is always best to solely focus in one location. The recommended locations for you to focus include areas, which include any food or water sources. Eventually, the moose will come out of their hiding places to hunt for food and water. By focusing on these food and water sources, you might just grab the chance to capture the moose when they are out searching for food and water.

Another tip for you is that you should make sure the clothing you are wearing for moose hunting will not make any or much noise when you move around. Moose are alert creatures that can be startled by any unknown noises and eventually, these noises will chase them away. In addition, it is advised that you should always be quiet when you are moose hunting. Noises will chase the moose away, causing you to be unable to even approach them, let alone capturing them.

If you discover a moose lurking around a certain area during the nighttime, do not be overexcited and launch a full attack on it because you might end up scaring it away. In this situation, you can mark down the location you saw the moose and come back in the morning. If the moose did not get shocked over the night, the possibility for it to return to the same location is higher and thus, this will be your chance to capture it when it reappears.

10. How to Go Bear Hunting

Bear hunting has been a hunting game that has gone down for generations. However, that doesn't mean anyone and everyone can go ahead and enjoy this sport, you need a license for the same and permission from the wildlife authorities to take part in this hunting sport.

The most important strategy used in bear hunting by most experienced hunters would be "spotting and stalking". This is done just as one would for any other hunting sport, but the distance here would be longer. When you spot and target a bear, you then decide to pursue the animal. This is when you start moving closer to the bear and try to test the acumen of the animal. Remember, the bear too is a hunter and would be very alert for any signs that he could pick up which spells trouble.

It is during the season of fall when bears usually start stocking up fat reserves by gorging on almost everything around them, especially fruits and nuts. So if you are actually searching for a bear to hunt during this season, it could be quite a challenging task to look for one if you are not in the right place where food sources are abundant.

Such food sources would be found especially during the summer scouting periods, and you should with your experience know when the right food sources would ripen and at which time of the year that is too in your area. Once you know this, then all you have to do is pick the right shootout point and find a nice hiding place. This would enable you to search for a bear sooner and finally get the animal down in one shot.

What you should learn about bear hunting is the behavior of bears. Try to smell the winds to check what the air currents are like at the time of the day you choose to hunt. If it is in the morning, you should smell upwards for signs and reverse for the afternoons to late evenings. To camouflage your presence, use the space around you, the trees or even other obstructions, which would block your presence from the senses of the animal altogether. Plus the terrain you choose to walk on can be challenging, beware of very steep terrains and those that have too much dry leaves and twigs around, noise should be avoided at all costs.

Don't use the predator call technique to attract the animal towards you. In addition, never go alone to hunt for bears. You would need more eyes to check around and if you are alone, there is always a danger of you being attacked by a bear or any other wild animal from behind.

Finally, getting down to the basics of bear hunting once again, it would take patience and time for you to have the right bear hunted down, so don't be in a hurry and come to play the sport with the whole day in mind.

11. How to go Bow and Arrow Hunting

A bow and arrow can mean miles existing between the hunt and the hunter. A single shot and it's all done. Bow and arrow hunting is so much popular among hunters all over the globe that it would really be a tough task to search for individuals who have never heard of bow and arrow hunting.

The most fascinating thing about a bow and arrow hunting is that it does not have any specific type of hunting that it is specialized in. A bow and arrow hunting is such a type of hunting that is flexible enough to suit hunting of all sorts of animals commencing from deer to bears.

A bow and arrow hunting is believed to have originated from the very ancient sport called Archery. Even epics do have archery engraved in them very clearly, which reflect a sign of warrior ship and respect. Nevertheless, only a few decades and archery has been transformed into what we call it today, bow and arrow hunting.

A bow and arrow hunting, today, is not just a sport to the hunters but it has become passion to the hunters. Whether it is hunting a white tail deer, a bear, and an elk or be it any form of bird, bow and arrow hunting is the most preferred means of hunting. A bow and arrow hunting not only provides a hunter the easiness of hunting at distance from the prey without getting noticed but also ensures the hunter to facilitate himself with a lot of safety measures which if avoided, at times, can prove to be fatal!

When it comes to a perfect bow and arrow hunting, a hunter should be very specific about his equipment. The equipment that a hunter should have could include compound bows, knives, bow sights, apparel, quivers, and arrows just to name a few. Firs, when on a bow and arrow hunt; one should set the values of his or her Bowstring's center or be it the value of loop height. It may be mentioned here that the bowstring's center serving and the string loop of an individual's bow controls the vertical alignments of the arrow availed in a specific bow.

The most important factor to be noted here is that if this alignment slips one bit, the accuracy of hunting will be suffer gravely. When specifying a perfect bow and arrow hunt, a perfectionist hunter makes it a habit of constantly checking the loop height with a T- square for accuracy.

Not only does this perfect hunter check for any loose joints in his bow and arrow. It must be mentioned here that a perfect loop height enables a hunter at least 15 feet above the ground level, thus facilitating suitable bow and arrow hunting.

12. THE BEST GUNS TO USE FOR HUNTING

If one of your favorite outdoor activities to conduct during your free time is hunting, you might have faced the frustration of choosing the best guns to use for these activities. Guns are important equipment one should equip in order to make the best out of the hunting activities they are conducting. Besides, the type of gun an individual uses for hunting also determines the success rate of the hunting activity. Thus, it is important for an individual to choose the most appropriate type of gun for the type of hunting activity he or she is going to participate in.

You should also bear in mind that different hunting activities require the equipment of different types of guns to maximize its success rate. Here are some guidelines for you to refer on the best type of guns to be used in different hunting activities. If you are planning to go deer hunting, the best guns for you to equip is the rifle, pistols, and shotguns. The rifle is ideal for short range shooting of the deer while both pistols and shotguns are optional guns to be used as backups for the rifle.

If you are planning to hunt for turkeys or pheasants, the shotgun might be one of the best choices of gun for you. However, the selection of the best guns for both turkey and pheasant hunting also depend heavily on your hunting style. If you are a skilled hunter of turkey or pheasant and you are able to aim well, the rifle would be your best choice of gun for this hunting activity. However, if you plan to launch a direct attack which involves the running up towards the turkey and the pheasant upfront, the shotgun, which is more appropriate to shoot in a close range setting, would be a more suitable choice for you.

Duck hunting is also one of the hunting activities that might require you to use a gun for a higher hunting success rate. There are a few types of guns for you to choose from, depending on your hunting style. First of all, you can choose to go with the shotgun. One of the best advantages of using a shotgun for duck hunting is the ability of the shotgun to withstand the worst situations and weather one might occur during the fun of the duck hunting activity.

There are also a few varieties of shotguns for you to choose from, ranging from the 10 gauge, 12 gauge, up to the 20 gauge shotgun. In order to select the best shotgun for you to use in your duck hunting activity, you might need to experiment with each of these shotguns first before you decide to use any of them.

13. HOW TO TRAP FOR ANIMALS

Always ensure you have a pair of latex gloves to wear. This is not only for your protection, but also to ensure you don't allow your body scent to be on the trap. Animals do have a strong sense of smell, even days after you laid the trap. Also while handling the bait; it would be wise not to allow your scent to be smothered over it.

Don't spend too much time around the trap. No spitting, smoking, touching, etc... Around where the bait is, and don't allow your pets to urinate or come close to the trap. Since the wild animals would have a strong sense of smell, they would use that tool to detect if humans are around or not. Choose the right location to have a successful catch, hence choose a place for the trap, which is secluded from human habitation.

Do not do this: Keep the trap where you can see it. Next to where the trash bins are, just because it comes to your bins every night. Remember, most animals are habitual in nature, which means they would use the same route and trail every day to come and go to their habitats. When you place the trap on one of these paths, it would be the best way to trap them.

Baits that you can use to trap animals: Bones, which have no meat on them. Good to lay them if you want to catch opossum, raccoons, coyote, skunk, feral hogs, large cats, and even wild dogs.

Sardines are best baits to catch armadillos, opossums, raccoons, large cats, coyotes and even feral cats. To catch feral hogs, skunks, raccoons or even opossums, you can use soured corn or plain corn as well.

Most would also use live bait, such as fish, rabbit, chicken and even small birds as well. This is indeed a good idea and works well when you want to trap wild animals that create a menace for you.

If you need any further help or if you are a novice at the game, it would be best to seek the help of an expert wild animal trapper. He or she would be able to best help you lay the trap and catch the annoying animal, which has made life hell for you.

14. How to hunt from a blind

A hunting blind is a mere covering device that is used frequently by expert hunters when it comes to hunting. A blind is designed mainly to prevent the detection of a hunter by its prey.

Duck blinds: Duck blinds are one of the most used types when it comes to blind hunting. These are mainly used in grain fields. What the hunter exactly does is that he or she runs into the grain field while tracking the prey.

Deer blinds: Deer blinds, though effective, yet are prohibited at many hunting areas. Therefore, before one tries to do this method, it is advisable to check the hunting laws or the rules and regulation of those areas. This mainly allows a hunter to build hiding places at a height from the ground level.

Camouflage blinds: This method enables a hunter to apply colors that may easily camouflage his construction thus facilitating the hunter to hunter at ease and in a perfect manner.

Tree stand blinds: This is the most traditional method and is allowed wherever hunting is allowed. This allows a hunter to hide himself behind some tree trunk in order to hide himself from his prey.

15. HOW TO GO FRESHWATER FISHING

If you like fishing and are looking for a sport that could last a whole year, try fresh water fishing. The best time to goes fresh water fishing and as many say, it gets better even better in the springtime. This is the time when the fish begin to spawn. In addition, just getting away from the rat race life that you might live, springtime fishing in fresh water would surely be a nice way to spend part of the day!

The lures used for fresh water fishing are just excessively many to choose from. This is when you have set your sights on the big catch and want to have the best show around. There are three important points when you go fresh water fishing next spring, so please read on and be well informed for the same.

The first point we would talk about is "top water": The water is very still and silent when it is very early in the morning and also very late in the evening. This is the time when the lure can be pulled out and used at your favorite watering hole, the lake or the pond to be precise. Lures as we all know are available in various ranges.

There are top water lures, which would rattle a little when the line is jerked. There are some, which would spin around the tail, or vibrate about when the spin is being reeled inwards. Finally, some lures would go crises cross when the reeling is done. No matter what type you choose, the lures of any type would be designed in such a way so that they attract the fish and make them bop on to the surface of the water body. This is where the fish would attack the lure and then slowly take it down with them.

The next point we would talk about is the "Soft Plastic Worm": If you use the famous Texas or the Carolina Jig with a worm as bait, you are assured of the fish biting it for a long time to come. The variety of scents and colors that are available for such a lure is wide and large to choose from. This is because the fish like a particular scent or color more than anything else. In addition, you should also keep in mind that while buying the lure, you have to check the time of the year when you are fishing or even the place. If you use a hook without weeds, the fish would be attracted faster.

Finally, we would like to tell you about the "Diving Jig": One of the most popular lures used for fresh water fishing by experts. It comes as a grub for the fish and would go down deep before coming back to the surface of the water. It would float at first when it is first put out there and when you reel quickly it would dive deep down. The moment you stop the reeling, it would ascend to the surface once again. The action is very closely mimicking the way the prey for freshwater fish behaves.

34

16. HOW TO GO TROUT FISHING

Having a great hobby is always a perfect way to pass time, especially when you are taking a break from a stressful workload and working environment. Depending on your interest, there are all sorts of different hobbies and activities you can choose from in order to make your free time meaningful. If you are a person with great patience and great determination, you can try out the hobby of fishing. In fishing, there are also different types of fishing styles that you can try to carry out. This article is on the fishing style of trout fishing.

Besides, of being a meaningful hobby for you to train your patience and determination, trout fishing is also a great hobby for those who have a desire for more adventurous experiences. Trout fishing is a fresh-water hobby, which is often being carried out near the river shores or on the mountain streams. One major condition for the stream or river that will contribute to the ideal spot for trout fishing is the altitude of the stream or the river. It is recommended that a fast and high altitude river or stream is the best spot for trout fishing.

Before departing for any trout fishing activity, you must also ensure that you have all the materials you need ready for the activity. The most important materials you must possess include rods, hook, line, spoon, and reel. Apart from that, it is also essential for you to make sure that your materials are all in the best condition to avoid any unwanted situation to happen when you carry out the activity of trout fishing, which will eventually lead to disappointment at the end of the day.

As mentioned, the location you choose for trout fishing is one of the most important factors you should consider before you depart for the location itself. The best location for trout fishing is the cold mountain streams. As for the ideal season for trout fishing, you would not need to worry about this because since trout fishing is a fresh water hobby, it directly means that the hobby can be carried out at any day or season of the year.

Similar to other fishing styles, the key to this hobby is patience. Remember not to make too much noise when you are trout fishing because this might eventually just scare the fishes away. Furthermore, you should also equip yourself as well as choose the ideal spot for trout fishing based on your personal budget and interest. You must also make sure that you obtain any necessary permits for the fishing spot you had chosen. Lastly, if you are a person who loves the Mother Nature and loves to be close to it, trout fishing might just be your next favorite hobby, which is both rewarding and meaningful.

17. How to go Bass Fishing

As the fast pace of our society keeps us all pretty busy, we find our time constantly being filled up with more workloads in order to adapt to the rapid changes in ever changing world we live in. However, no matter how busy we are, it is still encouraged for one to continue pursuing in things and activities they love. If you are into fishing or are planning to try out fishing for the first time as one of the activities you would like to practice during your free time, here are some tips on bass fishing that you might find pretty handy.

To help you understand the guidelines for bass fishing, this article will start off with a brief introduction of bass fishing as a whole. In short, bass fishing is usually being conducted in clear water areas. The baits that are to be used for bass fishing should always be dark in color. This is because bass fishing will be carried out in clear water areas. It is harder for the fishes in the water to become aware of light-colored baits, thus, causing the possibility of you catching any bass with light colored baits less likely, so stick to darker colored baits if you can.

In order to increase the rate in catching more fishes, the location for bass fishing to be carried out is one of the most important factors to be considered. Of course, there are some guidelines for you to refer to in order to choose the best location for bass fishing. First of all, you must know how to estimate the depth of the water. The temperature of the water is another aspect you must think about when choosing the best location for any bass fishing activities.

Another important factor for you to consider in increasing the catch rate is the baits you are using for the bass fishing activity. Bear in mind that the baits you will be using will be the main ingredient that will attract the fishes in the clear water area towards you. Thus, you must make sure that you are using the correct bait in catching the fishes. There are a few baits you can choose from to lure your target towards you. One of them is the Zara Spook. This bait looks almost like a cigar. The appropriate way to utilize this bait is to cast it out towards the clear water and pull it back slowly. The bait will then float on top of the water. Now, all you need to do is to wait for your bass to take your bait and start pulling your line.

Another type of bait you can use is the floating worm. The floating worm is a type of bait made with plastic and it creates an artificial outlook of the bait as a worm to trick the fishes in the clear water towards it, assuming the bait as their food. All you need to do is just to dip it in the water and wait for the fishes to take their bites at it, and hopefully you will catch a prize size fish!

18. How to go Catfish Fishing

A catfish is a kind of ray-finned type fish. The name comes from the shape of their prominent barbells that look like a cat's whiskers. Where to find them? So that you would know a nice secret location to do your catfish fishing.

An easy and convenient place to look for catfish is in three lakes. Besides, it is very fun when you go for the fishing activity and enjoyment. Do not presume that it would be a small catch. Actually, you can be able to get a big catfish, as long as your fishing skills are good or even professional.

You can find a variety of its species inside the lake. For example, they include channel cats, blue cats and flatheads as well as bullheads. You might not be familiar with some names. However, it is assured that they all are good to eat. Especially the smaller size ones are preferable because they get tougher when growing older and older.

A tip for you: catfish will normally hold along old creek and river channels in deep water inside lakes. Now, you should be smart to know where to hunt for them. They move shallow to feed, especially at night. It is their habitat. A clever fishing person will follow a creek channel across a flat to the back of a cove. Then you will unsurprisingly find catfish somewhere nearby it.

Besides, the water depth is another critical factor for catching catfish. During winter or summer, a group of catfish will hold in the deepest water. It is due to the volume of oxygen to support their living. Ironically, they will move to shallow water with hard bottoms to spawn during the springtime. How about the fall? They will move shallower because of the cooling water temperature on top, but then will go back deeper when it is getting colder and colder.

How about the suitable baits to use for catfish fishing? They usually will eat anything as long as they could get in their mouth. Therefore, liver, live minnows, crickets and earthworms will do as their attractive baits. You could hang the baits around and on hooks. Catfish are not a very smart fish at all. Even though you use those fake baits such as plastic worms, they will still make a hit and let you catch them easily.

In lakes, you can bait up a hole to draw them into a smaller area to trap and catch them. Besides, you should decide the size that you would like to catch. It will change the bait size and also rod type accordingly. It is common to use a six or seven foot medium action-spinning rod with a reel that has a good drag.

With the above tools and tricks, hopefully you could enjoy a big reward from catfish fishing activities. It is fun for family and friends, especially regarding how to spend your weekend, and if you love the taste of catfish, that is even better.

19. How to go Salmon Fishing

Salmon fishing can be one of the most fun types of fishing there is at times. If you want to spend your lazy weekend doing something fun to relax and unwind, we say salmon fishing is the way to go. But remember there are three stages to salmon fishing, that's if you want to really be successful at it.

Lake Fishing: When you fish in the famous great lakes, you should use a big boat. They would troll at a good speed and this is the best way to catch salmon with the help of down riggers. In these great lakes, there would be plenty of salmon feeding and they would hang around this place since the temperature of the water is perfect for the bait they would like to chew on. The down riggers should be brought deep into the water at 20 feet, and this is where you would find the majority of the salmon congregating for their bait. But in the summers, don't forget that you would have to go lower, probably around 150 feet or more, since the salmon go deeper and shallower on hot days.

River Fishing: In the beginning of fall or late summer months, it is at the river mouths where the salmon stage. The species wait for the rains to begin and to swell the water levels, so that they can go upstream for spawning. You can use various baits and lures at this point, since the fish are feeding as they swim upwards to spawn. But ensure that the fishing line is strong, since snagging can often happen. This is when the hooks come off the tail of the line and that even before the fish can grab the bait in its mouth, say experts.

Try using lures that don't vibrate and rattle too much, for this could annoy the school of salmon and they wouldn't want to come anywhere close to grab a bite, leaving you waiting for a very long time.

River Fishing Backwards: This is when the salmon now move upwards from the smaller streams. It is at this point when the feeding stops and ninety percent of the fish are caught by those who troll the waters. Remember that you need a license to fish legally, so ensure you get that before you go to the waters. The stage here is a time when the salmon have only one thing on their minds, which is to spawn. This is also a time when the salmon get very defensive about their territories and you would have to be very patient to catch a big one.

20. How to go Saltwater Fishing

If you are a person who is determined and patient, fishing might just be the ideal hobby for you. There are many types of fishing styles, which you can choose from based on your preference. In this article, the fishing style of saltwater fishing will be introduced and explained so as to help you in choosing the ideal fishing style for you by providing you with one of those options.

Instead of defining saltwater fishing as merely another hobby, saltwater fishing is also an adventure sport, which caters to individuals who are seeking for experiences that are more adventurous as well. This is because with saltwater fishing as a sport, one individual must not only face the huge and fierce fishes, but also the unfriendly and rapid water.

If you are new to saltwater fishing and you would like to start off with the basic steps for this sport, it is recommended for you to start off this hobby on the beaches, in which this spot will usually hold huge numbers of saltwater fish with the tide of the water being friendlier than the rapid streams.

If you are already familiar with the sport and would like to challenge yourself to another level, you can try saltwater fishing in the middle of the sea with your high-tech gear. By fishing in the middle of the sea, you will thus be able to face bigger saltwater fish, along with unpredictable rapid tides that might just approach you without any warnings in advance.

Being a professional in saltwater fishing, it is necessary for you to ensure that the gadgets you own are all usable in this activity. Some of the must-have gear includes the rods, nets, reels, pliers, gaffs, electronics, as well as proper clothing. Judging on the fact that the saltwater fishes might be more brutal due to the environment they are in, it is essential for you to make sure that all your equipment and gear are all in the best condition before you set of for saltwater fishing.

Of course, there are also a few tips or rules you can imply when carrying out the sport of saltwater fishing. One of them is to obey the rules of catch-and-release. One situation that allows you to keep the fish you capture is based on the injury they have when you catch them. If the fish is having an injury too serious for them to survive in the ocean, you might as well keep them for future uses.

Apart from that, it is also recommended that you can keep a fishing log with you, which you can record the process of your saltwater fishing every time you carry out this activity. This is important for you to recognize the behaviors of the fishes and thus, helping you in easing your saltwater fishing in the future. Important elements that you should be noting down include the moon phase, the weather, the tide phase, the cloud cover, the air and water temperature, as well as the wind speed and direction.

21. HOW TO GO TUNA FISHING

Fishing is a great past time hobby and many people are learning to appreciate this form of relaxing activity. Some people prefer to fish along the riverbanks or docks and there are people who love to sail into the sea to fish. If you prefer to fish along the riversides or by the docks, chances are the varieties of fishes that you will be able to catch are very limited.

The same cannot be said if you sailed out into the big ocean to fish. You will be surprised at the varieties of fishes that you will end up with at the end of the day. Of course, there is the chance that all your afternoon spent for nothing as you did not manage to catch anything but let's take our minds off from this pessimistic thought.

Tuna fishing is one of the activities that you can do out on the big ocean. Your chances of catching tunas are much higher out at the sea than by the riversides. It is often a very memorable experience to catch a tuna and it is especially true if it is your first attempt at tuna fishing.

Once you had your hands on tuna fishing, you will most likely be unable to go back to the ordinary fishing. However, as anglers around the world are committing the crime of overfishing, it has become a bit of a difficulty to actually catch any fish, what more of tuna. Therefore, you should learn some new tips to increase your chances of succeeding in tuna fishing.

The first thing you should know is that it is an art to know how to pick the right bait. Different baits work well on different types of fishes and not every fish will be attracted by the same bait. The same goes to what type of tuna breed you are trying to catch for each kind of tuna has its own feeding pattern. Therefore, you have to make sure you are using the right bait to catch the right fish or tuna. Other than that, you need to learn how to tie a good knot on your fishing rod.

Surely, you do not want to end up losing your catch of the day thanks to the faulty knot that you had tied. You also need to learn about ways to spot the location of tuna feeding and once you have mastered this skill, you will be able to catch tuna at any time and tuna fishing will be an easy thing for you.

22. How to go Tuna Fishing #2

Who wouldn't like to spend some nice time catching tuna? Yes, fishing has always been a relaxing sport, a recreation that helps you connect with nature and yet have loads of fun. But when you go out there to catch tuna, you need to bear some things in mind.

This is especially true when you want to come back home victorious and show off your talents and skills to everyone. Who doesn't want to photograph themselves with a big catch, we all do don't us? So today, we are going to give you some pointers to think of when you decide upon tuna fishing. Please read on and be well informed for the same.

The first thing you need to keep in mind would be the bait. You should know which bait would be most preferred by your friend, the tuna fish. The feeding habits for each tuna wouldn't be the same and hence you need to know which bait and under what conditions would the tuna be appealed to grab a bite.

Second thing to know would be the lure size and the type of lure to catch your tuna. Once again, the tuna is a very choosy fish and a lot would depend on the color and type of bait you would use to catch it.

Third point to remember would be the knots and rigs that you would use to catch the tuna fish. You don't have to spend a ton of money, only to know at the end that none of it works in your favor. You need to learn which are the best knots to use when you go tuna fishing.

The habits for feeding amongst the tuna fish are individualistic at the end of the day. This means you would be roaming around the waters all day long hoping for that big catch, but at the same time wouldn't know at what depths the fish feed or where they swim, what a waste!

You should also know where exactly to look for the tuna school of fish. When you know where they are, you would know where they feed and the signs would be clear for fishing thereof.

Take an online study or maybe get in touch with an expert with tuna fishing. Learn how the experts catch the big catch at the end of the day and sometimes in one shot. They have been doing it for a very long time now and wouldn't mind sharing a tip or two with you as well. Learn from the pros and maybe someday through the art of practice you would be in their shoes, teaching others as well.

Get in touch with fishing schools that train novice members like you maybe. They would have special classes, which would teach you techniques, and concepts to get your first big catch. The lessons are taught by pro anglers and they have caught big sized tuna's in the past. This is the best way to learn and go tuna fishing on that lazy Sunday afternoon!

23. How to go Sailfish Fishing

Chances are you should have seen at least a picture or a video of a man holding a big and heavy sailfish on a sailboat, a proud smile carved on his face. It seems such a great thing to do, sailfish fishing, especially watching that gleaming face of the man that you immediately want to go out into the ocean and start to sailfish fish. And you can be that man since all you have to do is just to own a good fishing rod and the right fishing skills and you are all set to go.

The first thing you should know is to learn about the types of sailfish. You should find out more information about how many types of sailfish are there around the location where you want to sailfish fish. Once you had learned all the things you should know about sailfish, then it is time to find out whether you are in the right season. Sailfish is just like a bird and it migrates according to season. Different seasons will lead to different type of sailfish being caught and you should know about this little piece of information.

The next thing to do is to secure the right bait. You should know that not all types of fish baits work on all kind of fishes. Those who had been fishing as hobby for a long time would have known this information but if you are new to the fishing game, you should consider thinking about what kind of fish you want to catch in the first place and then finding the right bait to do so. Certain bait might work well on certain types of sailfish but it might turn off others on reasons such as colors being too bright or dull, the shapes being not appealing enough, and so on. Therefore, you should do some studies on this aspect of fishing first hand before actually sailing out to fish.

Maybe after you had learned all you need to learn, then you are ready to go out into the sea and start sailfish fishing. You had secured the boat to sail out into the sea and are all set with the right bait and the right equipment. And you did manage to catch a sailfish when you are out on the sea. But the question now is how you are going to transfer your catch into your boat? Make sure all these questions are answered before going sailfish fish.

24. How to go Shark Fishing

Many people often thought that sharks are one of the most dangerous animals on the planet, no thanks to the devilish portrayal in the classic movie, Jaws, by Steven Spielberg. While it is no doubt that sharks are able to bring death to humans, it is actually quite a misunderstood creature for it is a very gentle sea animal and more often than not, it is them that are more afraid of us than we of them whenever we are at the sea. After all, who is not to be afraid of us humans, when we are constantly doing shark fishing and poaching this beautiful animal?

Shark fishing has become a widely practiced activity because there is a great demand for this sea animal. There are many people who are willing to pay a hefty amount of money in order to have a taste of shark meat. It is especially true in Asia countries where shark fins are widely in demand due to its status as a rich people's food. In Hong Kong and China, shark fins are a form of delicacies that are savored by the citizens regularly and this has caused the increase of people involving in shark fishing.

Generally, there is no concrete answer as to what attracts sharks to take the bait you used for shark fishing. No doubt, that the presence of blood will greatly enhance the chances of them taking the baits but it is not a guarantee that bloods will attract this sea creature. Usually, it is the combinations of blood and other factors that will excite the animals and attract them to attack. It goes without saying that the more dangerous the sharks are, the harder it will be to capture it. Great white sharks, bull sharks, tiger sharks and many more are just some of the species that are well known for its aggressiveness.

Shark is one of the many endangered sea creatures that are constantly being hunted for the wrong reason. Shark fishing should not exist for the sake of appeasing to our appetites to exotic meats. Hence, many countries are working to ban shark fishing in order to protect this sea creature from being extinct permanently of the face of the earth. We can also do our part in helping to protect these delicate animals by not eating shark fins or shark meats.

25. How to go Crab fishing

Generally, crab fishing is a way in which a fishery catches or farms crabs. Now, the Discovery Channel has posted a piece of interesting facts about crab fishing, specifically for Alaska country. It has referred to the crab fisheries as the deadliest catching job. Why do you ask?

It is a seasonal business. The most lucrative period for Alaskan crab fishing is during the fall and winter. For example, the two most active months for the Bering Sea are October and January. Unfortunately, both are short seasons, mere lasting less than four weeks. It is yet lucrative within a four-week month for the angler.

For each season, a total of 250 crab fishing boats are approximately estimated to converge on Dutch Harbor, Alaska. Do you know they are hunting for Alaskan king crab? Crabs do have many different species, such as flower crab, snow crab, blue crab and so on. And, these 250 boats are only in search for the King Crab, which measures 6.5 inches.

Despite the knowledge of different crab types, you would be amazed by the building cost of crab vessels. It can cost up to several million dollars to build a crab fishing boat. Besides, the operational cost is roughly around tens of thousands of dollars. Therefore, this crab fishing trade must be very profitable to do so.

For the boats, they are ranged in size from 40 to 200 feet long. Also, each catching crew would systematically consist of one captain and three to nine deckhands. They will risk health and safety issues during the catching to a certain extent of danger harm.

Furthermore, most fishing boats will have downward-pointing sonar. Notice that it is downward pointing. It, thus, would not detect crabs that are right against or buried in the ocean floor.

To catch adult male crab, the captain must be very capable and have a good super-natural intuition. It is because the sonar would not possibly be able to predict their location. Only the exceptional case occurs in spring season, which is the mating season.

Anglers will use 700-pound steel traps or pots baited with ground herring, squid, sardines and cod, at least 400 feet below the ocean's surface. They are ideal to attract and catch crabs. However, as they try to get to the bait, those crabs will injure each other. It is very cruel to see a seriously injured crab as bait for the other crabs to eat as well. The pots normally measure 7 feet by 7 feet by 3 feet. It soak anywhere from five to 24 hours before being hauled back on deck.

26. How to go Lobster fishing

Everyone will be licking their fingers when having lobsters on their dinner table. It is not cheap but very delicious seafood. Lobster fishing starts its trend when human beings have discovered that it is a yummy meal.

Today, it is a very profitable business venture for an angler, and a country. However, before it would require high capital outlay for expensive fishing gear and, of course, a nice fishing boat. The sea is very unpredictable, more than the weather. When you are out lobster fishing, you are risking your life.

How to kick start this lucrative sea venture? First, you would need to have a lobster fishing license and permit. Remember, it is always uneasy as long as the task is about getting a license. For example, Maine has a state license and a federal license. The federal license is a permission to catch the lobsters in the winter, while the state license is a fishing permission for specified state-regulated fishing season. Overall, you need to make clear about the laws and regulations about lobster fishing in your country, since every country is different in this aspect.

As stated above, a hardy boat is necessity and an essential. You can look for it through the classifieds or online, such as dealers or your connections from other fishing boat owners. Do not purchase a boat because of an attractive price tag alone.

Make sure you get insurance for your boat and the crew. After that, you would start to gather all the necessary fishing gear. As a rule, you will probably need two buoys per line. If you have 10 lines, you will need to purchase 20 buoys and 100 traps. Now, you should fix the number of lines you would desire to set up. It would depend on fishing alone or in a team. Of course, you could not forget a gaff to pull the buoy in.

It is almost similar to driving, you would like to have one GPS unit to guide and direct you throughout the big sea. For example, the GPS could help you to locate your lines and also enable you to set your engine on autopilot as you steam between lines.

Communication devices, such as a radio, play a role to communicate with the Coast Guard and other vessels as well. Besides, weather gear like waterproof boots, warm coats, sweaters, hats, gloves, and dry socks, should be always ready available inside your boat, even as a backup when you get wet out on deck.

You should have an idea as to where to buy your bait, keep your boat, and also who to buy your lobster products. You could direct sell your catch to restaurants, or to companies that export or sell lobster locally. Talk to other angler about where they sell their catches at, and have fun.

27. How to Go Fly Fishing

Have you ever thought of fly-fishing when planning for a weekend or holiday vacation to get away and have some fun? Fly fishing is not fishing for flies. Fly-fishing is an angling method in which an artificial "fly" is used to catch fish.

Today, it is one of the fastest growing leisure sports. Besides, it is also conserving natural resources as well as supplying aquatic recreation for people. Sounds as 1-2-3, a person should have three essential equipment's to start their fly-fishing. They are rod, line, and casting technique. You must ensure that they must exist together so that you could have a good catch.

If you are a beginner in this fishing activity, you might contemplate whether what kinds of fishing rod for flies to use for your fishing. Hollow glass is preferable to be the beginner's choice, rather than bamboo. It requires less care and will not take a set if improperly handled or stored. A nice suitable fishing rod is definitely critical for fly-fishing. Without the right rod, it would be very hard to enjoy the fun and reward from the activity of fly-fishing.

Secondly, the line must be a good match with your rod. Otherwise, your line would be too light to bring out the rod action. You should get a C level, an HCH double taper or a GBF three-diameter. Most of them will work best with their rod partner, regardless of lengths or weights. If you feel strange, kindly visit one of the fishing stores in your area and ask more about it. They would teach you to pick up the perfect line for your light rod. It would better to gain much knowledge about fishing equipment's before getting involved in fly-fishing.

Speaking about casting techniques, it is important to get about 20 feet of line out front. Remember, a straight-line casting is the perfect fishing technique. How to make it? First, you must let yourself relaxing fully. Taunt muscles will ruin all the things, specifically your casting movement.

Many people are enjoying their fly-fishing time out on the water. You could be one of them, as long as you start to use these skills. The above three points are the most fundamental ones. Not only for fly-fishing, but also it could be for other types of fishing activities. A solid fishing foundation is very important and not allowed to be neglected.

Right now, what you should do is choose a good location and some fishing partners if you want to, such as a friend who has lots of experience in fly-fishing. After that, you should spend a day fishing on that site to learn casting. Even practicing casting is a fun experience.

28. How to go Spear Fishing

Being able to do something you like during your free time is one of the best times you can obtain in the midst of your busy schedule. There are many hobbies one can practice during their free time, depending on the personality and interests of the individual. If you are interested in fishing, here are some tips and guidelines for spear fishing that can assist you in advancing towards the accurate step for this leisure pursuit.

Spear fishing, unlike any other types of fishing methods, possesses a higher degree of difficulty. Besides, spear fishing is also more challenging than the other fishing methods. You can refer to some of these tips to get you started. First of all, before you start your expedition towards the activity of spear fishing, you must always make sure that you have prepared the best and most appropriate equipment and tools needed for this activity. However, it is also not recommended for you to bring along too much equipment and tools in the same time as it might cause hindrance for your spear fishing activity and it might disturb you from enjoying the beauty and serenity of the underwater world as well.

Before you head out for any spear fishing activity, you must also make sure that you are physically fit first. This is because spear fishing is an activity that demands individuals to be physically fit. Being physically fit means that you will be able to endure the pressure in the water and thus, prolong your excitement and enjoyment underwater. If you are unable to stay underwater for a long time, it might not only cause you to be less excited with spear fishing, but it might also affect your health in the same manner.

Furthermore, it is also extremely important for you to conduct a certain extent of research first before you started off with the activity of spear fishing. You need to be sure with the location you choose, in terms of the water temperature, the depth of the water and so forth. This is important for you to be able to choose the best tools and equipment you will be bringing together with you in conducting the activity of spear fishing. In the same time, you must also find out about the rules and regulations of the spot you had selected so that you would not get yourself into trouble, which will really put a damper on your spear fishing excitement.

One of the most important pieces of items you must not forget to bring along with you is a short knife. When you are diving underwater, it is undeniable that there might be certain unknown elements appearing before you, such as entanglements. Thus, it is important for you to always equip yourself with a short knife when you go spear fishing so that you will be able to eliminate any obstacles in front of you or even protect yourself when necessary, especially when you are faced with certain threats that might endanger your life.

29. How to go Ice Fishing

Ice fishing is a popular sport for the folks who reside in the northern regions. The sport is an excellent and a very beneficial way to unwind and relax. With the rat race world we live in, who wouldn't like to spend some quality time, doing what you like the best, which is ice fishing? This is also a time when family and friends can gather along the icy shores and spend quality time with one another.

The lures for quality ice fishing are plenty to choose from. There are even many baits as well as fishing tools to help you have fun and succeed with a big catch at the end of the day. Keep reading to learn about the basics of ice fishing and how you can get started with this fun relaxing sport, so grab your long underwear and learn more.

Just like in any other sport, you need to be dressed appropriately for this fun outdoor activity. This means you would be on the ice and hence dress warmly for the occasion. You should have enough layers on you to maintain your body temperature.

Before you go ice fishing, do make sure to visit the local sports store in your area. Over there you would find plenty of fishing tools and equipment to make the catch memorable. They would also tell you about the best bites, which bait you, should buy and use, and also which spots for ice fishing you should go to.

Don't forget, just as in any other sport, which would mean hunting down species; you would need a license to fish, so ensure that you have it on you. And once this is done and is in place, make sure your bags are packed. In the bags, you should have your fishing pole and line, a bucket for the bait, an ice auger, lures, bait, towels, bench, and a tool to measure the depth, water and food for your needs.

Check the condition of the ice before you step on it, sometimes the thickness can be deceiving. The ice as experts say should be around four to five inches thick, hard and well frozen. Remember the depth of snow right on top would be of no value.

At the venue, find a nice place somewhere close to where the other anglers are. Remember the local know the area in and out and would be of help to tell you where the best bites would happen.

Using the ice auger make a hole and take out as much of the ice pieces as possible, because if there are pieces that float they could break the line you use. The next thing to do is to use the net when the line is being baited on. This way you can ensure your hands stay dry.

The line should be weighed since you would want to fish close to the lake's bottom. The warmer parts of the lake would always be at the bottom and that's where the fish would also be. Finally, be patient and if the fish don't bite where you are, move a little bit more away and try there.

Vince Stead has been raising dogs for over 25 years now, and served in the United States Navy for 8 years from 1982 to 1990. He has worked for himself for the last 20 years, and lives in Southern California.

OTHER BOOKS BY VINCE STEAD

Sammy the Runaway Mastiff
ISBN# 1-59824-314-4

The Back Yard Kids Club
ISBN# 978-1456406219

How to Get Even and Revenge with Pranks on Anyone
ISBN# 978-1-45387-727-2

Navy Fun
ISBN# 978-1-59824-514-1

Navy Sea Stories
ISBN# 978-1456558666

Look for dog-breed training books written by Vince Stead.

Made in the USA
San Bernardino, CA
20 February 2016